LOOK AHEAD

a guide to
working in...

Sport

Alan Vincent

Heinemann

www.heinemann.co.uk
Visit our website to find out more information about **Heinemann Library** books.

To order:
☎ Phone 44 (0) 1865 888066
 Send a fax to 44 (0) 1865 314091
💻 Visit the Heinemann Bookshop at www.heinemann.co.uk to browse our catalogue and order online.

First published in Great Britain by Heinemann Library, Halley Court, Jordan Hill, Oxford OX2 8EJ, a division of Reed Educational and Professional Publishing Ltd. Heinemann is a registered trademark of Reed Educational & Professional Publishing Limited.

OXFORD MELBOURNE AUCKLAND JOHANNESBURG BLANTYRE
GABORONE IBADAN PORTSMOUTH NH (USA) CHICAGO

Designed by Ambassador Litho
Illustrations by
Originated by Ambassador
Printed in Hong Kong/China

ISBN 0 431 094845 (Hardback)   ISBN 0 431 09490 X (Paperback)
04 03 02 01 00   05 04 03 02 01
10 9 8 7 6 5 4 3 2 1   10 9 8 7 6 5 4 3 2 1

British Library Cataloguing in Publication Data
Vincent, Alan
         A guide to working in sport – (Look ahead)
         1.Sports – Vocational guidance – Great Britain
         I. Title II.Sport
         796'.02341

Acknowledgements
The Publishers would like to thank the following for permission to reproduce photographs: Action-plus, pp. 15/Chris Barry, 20/Chris Brown, 30/, 44/Glyn Kirk, 46/Neil Tingle; Allsport, pp. 9/Shaun Botterill, 18/David Cannon, 25/Mark Thompson, 28/Dave Rogers, /52 Clive Brunshill; Barking Abbey Comprehensive School, p. 33; Denis Kennedy, p. 55; Empics, pp. 13/Tony Marshall, 17/John Marsh, 41/John Buckle; Heinemann/Trevor Clifford, p. 37; Kit Houghton, p. 23; National Coaching Federation, p. 40; Nick Hamilton/Whitelines Magazine, p. 5; Photodisc, p. 7 (all); Robert Ashton, p. 5; Stone, p. 48/Christopher Bissell; Tony Stone Images/Paul Harris, p. 26; Tony Tickle, p. 5; University of Stirling, p. 36.

Cover photograph reproduced with permission of Sporting Pictures.

Our thanks to Joanna Dring, careers co-ordinator, Banbury School, Oxon for her help in the preparation of this book.

Every effort has been made to contact copyright holders of any material reproduced in this book. Any omissions will be rectified in subsequent printings if notice is given to the Publisher.

Contents

Technical words, jargon and specialist terms are explained in the glossary.

[The glossary also includes explanations of the acronyms (abbreviations) of associations and organizations mentioned in the text].

Get real!

An introduction to working in sport

So, you're interested in the world of sport? This book will help you to think clearly about that interest … whether or not you decide to pursue it further, you need to be sure of all the angles. You need to have a real picture of what it's like to be involved in a career in sport, what the prospects are, and the sort of things you need to take into account – before you commit yourself.

Along the way, you will find a lot of information and practical tips to help you make up your mind – and take some initial steps.

These first few pages set the scene, so you can look at the general picture facing you or anyone who might want to work in sport or in a sports-related job.

'Earning from playing' (pages 8–31) is where you will find more detailed information about specific sports. This section is likely to be of particular interest if you are already showing signs of exceptional talent or interest in one of the sports listed and want to know more about that sport and the opportunities it may offer. Case studies are included, to show how some people have made it in their own ways.

'How to break in' (pages 32–38) talks about the various ways that you can get into a job or career in these same sports. This supplements the information given alongside job entries in the other sections.

Next, in 'Sports-related jobs and careers' (pages 39–53), there is a look at a wide range of job and career opportunities in sport that do not involve being a sportsman or woman as such.

'What then?' (pages 54–55) is an important reminder that, even for those few who do reach the top in sport, life has to carry on after the active career has ended. Here you can look at some of the opportunities open to sportsmen and women who can no longer earn their living from active performance in sport.

The 'Useful information, addresses & contacts' pages (starting on page 56) list the addresses and contact details of the relevant governing bodies, associations and agencies. These organizations may be able to supply you with useful careers information, as well as details of specialist magazines which often carry job adverts. You could also contact the organizations to find out about education and training opportunities.

Finally, there is a glossary of terms used in the text and an index to help you find your way around the book.

⭐ *There is a huge range of sports in which people compete professionally. Find out as much as possible about the sports you are most interested in if you think you might want to make a career in one of them.*

Sport – an overview

Approximately half a million people work in the sport and fitness industry, but relatively few are professional sportsmen and women. Many sports make use of part-time professionals, who may well need to do another job to make a reasonable living.

There will continue to be more opportunities in sports and leisure, as it is a growth industry. Expansion is most rapid in the private sector, and it is happening particularly in health and fitness, outdoor activities and development training.

Do you match up?

If you are really determined to be one of the few who do make a living out of sport, you need to make a realistic self-assessment. You also need to be sure of your own motivation and ability.

In terms of skill and talent, how do you compare with other young people? If the sport you are most interested in is played at school, your PE teacher can give you some idea of whether you have the exceptional talent to make it as a paid sports player. Outside school, your club coaches will have a good idea of how you compare with other young people in the area, regionally or nationally.

Never underestimate how competitive sport is. The young person who does make it will always have shone, although maybe not as the most outstanding player: motivation and perseverance are important factors in all sports.

Sport at the top level is now part of the entertainment and media industries. Intense media coverage can lead to unrealistic expectations in some young people. Always remember that relatively few people make a comfortable living out of their sport.

Newspapers and TV can also exaggerate the glamour of sport at the top. Top tennis players and footballers have to find ways of killing the boredom of time spent between training sessions and matches. There can be a lot of drudgery and routine in carving out a career in sport. Nigel Mansell, one of Britain's most successful racing drivers, spent many 'lean years' before making it to the top.

You may already have decided that you want to work in sport but not as a professional player. In many jobs, you will need some sporting talent as well as enthusiasm. In most jobs related to sport, there are other skills and qualities that you will need if you are to succeed. Initiative, adaptability and the ability to function well in a team are usually crucial. You will also need good communication and inter-personal skills. Specific jobs will require other skills, for example in business practice, information technology or languages. Even where such skills are not essential, they are likely to help progress in a very competitive career field.

⭐ *Whatever your sport you need dedication, motivation and perseverance, as well as talent, to make sport a career.*

Earning from playing – an A–Z of sports

Media coverage tells us which sports offer most full-time career opportunities. Football dominates the sports pages of our newspapers for ten months of the year, with other sports vying for the scraps. Some of the richest sports, such as motor racing, have very few full-time professionals.

Even for the professionals, levels of financial reward vary enormously. A few are set up for life and don't need to worry about a job beyond their active sporting careers. This happens more in the sports that benefit most from sponsorship or high public interest, such as golf, soccer and tennis. Many more earn a reasonable living, others earn only some financial support. For some, following a sporting interest full-time may actually mean being worse off financially.

ELITE
TOP
EARNERS

FULL TIME
PLAYERS WHO
EARN A MODERATE
INCOME FROM THEIR
SPORT

PART-TIMERS WHO DRAW
SOME INCOME FROM THEIR
SPORT

FUN PERFORMERS WHO MAY PICK UP
OCCASIONAL WINNINGS FROM
COMPETITION

This pyramid shows the relatively few top earners, compared to the number of people who earn very little from sport.

The growth of, and changes in, sport and leisure have led to more people being able to earn some money from participating in sport. You can earn money from tournament or competition wins, coaching, exhibitions, media fees, sponsorship and equipment fees. At the higher levels, there are sometimes grants from the Lottery Sports Fund, while other grant sources are the Sports Aid Foundation, sports councils, local authorities or company sponsorship schemes. But all these sources still create relatively few opportunities for the full-time professional.

Here are some of the sports which do offer opportunities for paid professionals, with information on how you can best break in.

Athletics

It's possible for a few performers to receive great financial rewards. The fastest sprinters in the world can negotiate something like £60,000 for a single meeting – where their race is over in a fraction less than ten seconds!

⭐ *Marion Jones is the fastest woman athlete in the world and one of the sport's top earners.*

The insurance company CGU has recently put £10 million into athletics. In 1999 UK Athletics signed a deal with the BBC worth £17 million over five years and secured another £2.8 million in National Lottery Funding from Sport England.

High-profile athletes like Steve Backley and Paula Ratcliffe are full-time athletes and earn a good living. Across each individual event, the governing body is able to offer some financial subsidy to ranked athletes, though this is nothing like a living wage.

Getting in

At present the grants and scholarships available just help with the costs of travel and equipment. You need to work your way up through the junior ranks, with the bigger rewards only becoming available at under-20 or under-23 level, and only for the highest achievers.

Several universities act as High Performance Centres. As well as its degree courses, Bath University runs an HND course in Coach Education & Sports Performance. Scholarship awards are available to high performers.

Perriss Wilkins – making it as a full-time athlete

Perriss Wilkins is the British record holder for the discus. He has been throwing since the age of 14, when injury stopped him playing rugby for a couple of years. He was always a talented thrower, but only came through to the top in his late twenties, after he committed himself to a full winter's conditioning and training programme. He decided then to aim for a place at the Sydney Olympics in 2000.

The transition to becoming a more-or-less professional thrower was not an easy one and Perriss almost became bankrupt in the early stages. He had to take more time off work, without pay, to accommodate the additional training and competition and he was having to pay out more on food, equipment, training, massage and other specialist support.

He turned the corner in 1997, when he broke the British record, which gave him his first taste of Lottery funding, along with vouchers for physiotherapy and medical back-up. In Perriss's case, Lottery money is supplemented by additional monthly payments from an independent sponsor, who also gives him some help with accommodation.

After the European Championships in 1998, Perriss knew he had to become a full-time athlete if he was going to enjoy further success. This was the right moment for him, but he stresses, *'It's a mistake to go full-time unless you're at the very top and needing to compete two or three times a week.'*

Perriss hopes to compete at top level until the Commonwealth Games in 2002, but is also planning his career beyond that. Taking advantage of what spare time he has and using the voucher system, he has taken courses in coaching, massage and weightlifting and expects to take a job in coaching, probably in Canada, which, like the USA, offers many opportunities in the college system.

Perriss did not achieve many qualifications at school and says to any up-and-coming athletes, *'Don't be put off by people who put you down, even if you're not good at school, you can use athletics to get a career.'*

⭐ *Perriss Wilkins showed great courage and determination on the way to achieving his athletic dream.*

Basketball

The national league has more than 60 clubs, with men's, women's and junior men's divisions, but there are still very few professional players from the UK.

Getting in

You need to find a local club – or quite possibly one further afield – if you are to reach the standards of excellence needed to exploit the few opportunities. The bigger clubs run junior or cadet teams. Some of the best players take up opportunities to study and sharpen their skills at American universities. Height is a definite advantage and many players are well over 2 metres (6 feet 7 inches) tall.

Billiards and snooker

Television exposure and sponsorship have led to increasing opportunities in a sport that has a long record of professionalism. As with darts and motor racing, there is some concern about the need to replace income from cigarette company sponsorship, once legislation to limit this takes full effect.

The number of players entitled to play in professional tournaments is controlled by the world governing body – there are currently about 600 professionals. As with many other sports, the professionals can supplement their tournament winnings with income from exhibition matches and personal appearances. Several also run their own clubs.

Getting in

Promotion to the professional ranks is on a competitive basis, with the top amateurs competing with each other and with the lower ranked professionals to make it to senior level.

Good technical ability and a successful tournament record are the essential ingredients for a young player who wishes to become a professional. There are a number of professional managers who recruit potential circuit players at an early age. The World Professional Billiards and Snooker Association has coaching schemes for young players.

Boxing

The continued risk of injury and even death has worked with a small number of high-profile scandals to turn public opinion against boxing. Yet it continues to provide

Paul Hunter demonstrates the technique that took him to the World Snooker Championships in 1999.

career opportunities for a small number of professional boxers. There are several hundred licensed boxers, but only a small proportion make a reasonable living.

HAVE YOU THOUGHT OF...

- WRITING TO THE GOVERNING BODY FOR YOUR SPORT
- CONTACTING OTHER RELEVANT ORGANIZATIONS
- CHECKING OUT THE BEST WEBSITES
- ASKING FOR AN INTERVIEW WITH YOUR CAREERS ADVISER?

There is something of a gulf between the recognized governing body and the body that controls the professional branch of the sport. The Amateur Boxing Association is recognized by the UK Sports Councils for development and promotional purposes, but at professional level it is the British Boxing Board of Control that provides the administration.

Getting in

You need to join a club that offers good, safe training for young boxers. Professional managers sometimes sign up promising young boxers from the age of 17, but most boxers take the amateur route until at least 20. They then become eligible to fight in major tournaments. Either way, you have to apply to the British Board of Boxing Control to become a professional. This entails an interview and a thorough medical examination.

Cricket

In England at least, cricket is a major sport, with TV coverage and sponsorships, yet comparatively few opportunities. From 2000 there are two sections of the County Championship with 18 teams competing: this means there will be some 400–450 players on professional contracts. There are also some part-time professionals, playing in Minor Counties cricket, county and Scottish leagues.

County cricket only operates for about five months of the year and the players often need to find other work during the remainder of the year. This may mean playing or coaching abroad or taking alternative employment, usually outside sport.

Getting in

All the major counties have selectors who watch school and local club matches and invite talented young players to trials. The best are invited to play a few matches for the county second XI. They play part-time until they are offered a summer contract and a place on the playing staff. The Marylebone Cricket Club (MCC) runs a scheme offering three summer sessions with study for an Advanced GNVQ in Leisure and Recreation.

⭐ *Action from an under-15s cricket match.*

Cycling

The sport's popularity in Britain cannot compete with its status in mainland Europe. The Tour de France is the annual long-distance road race that provides an amazing and varied spectacle for huge numbers of spectators and television viewers. The organizers say it is the world's third largest sporting event, after the Soccer World Cup and the Olympics: it has a budget of £25 million and involves about 3700 people. In the UK there are only about 70 professional riders, some of them working abroad as members of sponsored teams.

Getting in

Entry to the professional ranks is usually through success as an amateur rider. You need to join a local cycling club and make rapid progress through competition. There are 26 geographical divisions to oversee the clubs and competition in England, with separate organizations in Scotland and Wales.

Remember to keep your general fitness levels up. Successful cyclists do other training, including running, gym work and weightlifting.

Darts

Darts is another sport that has developed considerably through the involvement of TV and sponsors. Only the top few players earn a full living from tournaments and exhibitions, but many more supplement their main income with winnings in local and regional leagues and tournaments.

Getting in

Exceptional technical skill, concentration, good nerves, consistency and showmanship are the elements which mark out the few who make it to the top-earning levels in the sport. While individual practice is the key to progress, young darts players need to test their competitive temperament and can do this by working their way up through local pub and club teams.

Football

Soccer currently reigns supreme in British sport. In other sports only the really major championships can attract the sort of publicity regularly available to soccer.

There are some 2500 full-time soccer professionals in the UK, more than in any other sport. There are also approximately 1500 part-timers and 300 youth trainees. Most are employed by the 130 Football League and Scottish League clubs, although sponsorship from local business now sees wages of up to £400 per week for some players in other leagues (Nationwide Conference, Dr Martens, Ryman, Unibond). Football is no longer a seasonal job for the top players, whose only holiday may be one month in the summer. Fitness and tactical training and matches continue all year round, even over bank holidays and Christmas.

The next few years are likely to see further changes in the sport, driven by its continuing popularity and commercial success. The prospects for British-born players may be boosted by substantial investment from the Premiership in schools and local club football.

See also the Football Association's publication, *Football as a Career*.

Getting in

Talented young players are usually spotted by club scouts. They join Football Academies or Centres of Excellence associated with FA Premier League and Football League clubs. Young players aged 9–16 attend training sessions two or three nights a week. At 16, they may be invited to become full-time trainees. They also do routine work, such as cleaning dressing rooms and boots. Young entrants have to attend college part-time to gain further qualifications. At 17 or 18 years old, those who have a good chance of making it to the top level are offered a full-time contract.

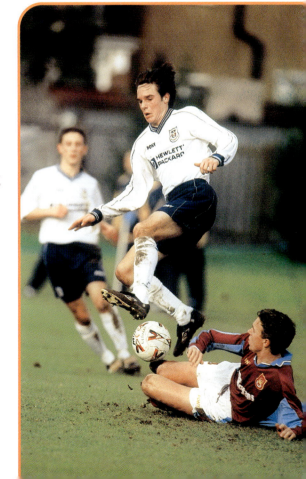

⭐ *These young players are already attached to top league clubs.*

A small number of 14/15-year-olds are selected for the fast-track route to professional football, the Football Association's National School of Excellence at Lilleshall in Shropshire. Here, young players receive specialist tuition, while attending local schools.

Few footballers in the UK have had a university education, but for students of the game there is a Science & Football degree course at Liverpool John Moores University and an HND equivalent at Southwark College in London.

Golf

Few players earn their living on the professional tournament circuit – about 250 men and 100 women. Golf has, however, benefited from the movement towards merchandising, with huge, world-wide sales of equipment and clothes. Corporate activity, with many business companies favouring the sport as a focus for rewarding their own employees or entertaining their clients, has also brought opportunities in **marketing** and **retail**, as well as in the traditional role of **club professional**.

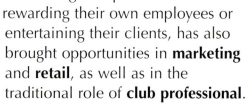

The ambitious must start young in golf.

There are some 2200 club professionals in the UK (only 30–40 of them women), employed by private and public sector clubs. The role of the club professional is to teach and play with club members and visitors, but also to run the club shop and repair and maintain equipment. The club professional's income is therefore likely to be made up of a 'retainer' paid by the club, supplemented by earnings from teaching fees, shop sales and repairs.

Getting in

To compete in a professional tournament, golfers must obtain a 'player's ticket' through good results in local competitions. This usually means playing to an extremely high standard. The player's ticket allows entry to one of the two pre-qualifying events. Some 130 players go on to a larger European tournament of 250–300 players, held in Spain. About 50 are then able to progress to the professional European circuit.

Becoming a club professional requires a handicap of four or better. You also need at least four GCSEs at grade C or above, Intermediate GNVQ or NVQ level 2 (or Scottish equivalent level 2 qualifications). You start out being contracted to a club professional and work in the club shop, selling and repairing equipment and helping with the office work. Young entrants may also be asked to coach club members.

After a six-month probationary period as an assistant professional, you are eligible for the Professional Golfers' Association (PGA) training scheme, which involves a minimum of three years' training. It combines distance learning with residential courses at the PGA's training academy at the Belfry, Sutton Coldfield. This diploma course gives a thorough grounding in teaching golf, exercise and fitness, marketing and retailing, and business and practical skills. Those who are successful take up jobs as club professionals in the UK and abroad, in corporate golf or retail, or occasionally in the media.

The PGA has a video, *What does it take to become a PGA professional?*, about its diploma programme. The English Golf Union also has a careers leaflet, *An Introduction to Education and Career Opportunities in Golf.*

Women in sport

There are fewer opportunities for women than for men in professional sport. Traditional attitudes have held up women's progress in many sports such as cricket, golf and soccer. In athletics, some disciplines have only recently been opened up to women and only in 1999 the Football Association was fined for refusing to accredit female coaches with its coaching licence.

While active discrimination gradually lessens (or is contained by regulation), the barriers that remain are often more about the economic realities. With more men watching and playing sport, the financial rewards tend to be far greater for men. Nevertheless, rapid progress has been made in recent years.

The situation is much healthier for women in other sports-related careers, for example in administration and in health and fitness. Here the skills that women offer are widely valued and more of them are finding worthwhile jobs and careers.

The Institute of Leisure and Amenity Management, with the support of the Women's Sports Foundation and Sport England, offers training courses for women already working in the sports sector.

The Women's Sports Foundation itself does outstanding work in promoting and supporting the role of women in sport. It offers information days on employment opportunities and a personal development course, 'Get Set, Go!', to help young women become sports leaders.

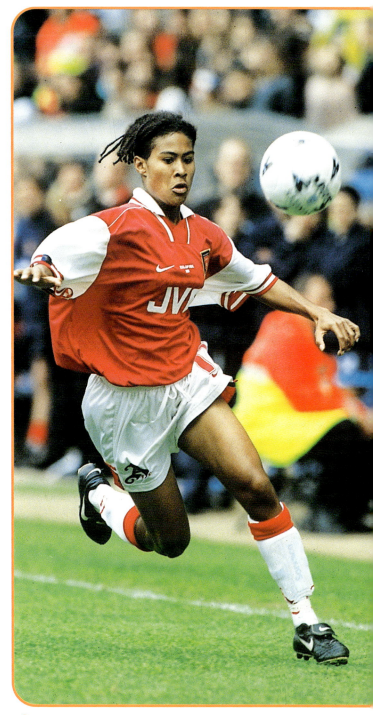

⭐ *Women's football is reaching new standards of excellence and increasing in popularity.*

Horse racing

There are about 120–130 flat-race **jockeys** and 400 in National Hunt (over jumps). The flat season is from March to November. National Hunt racing takes place throughout the year. Jockeys are paid a riding fee and also receive a percentage of any winnings.

Pay for **trainee jockeys** and **stable hands** is usually in the range £100–£200 per week, with accommodation often provided. With early mornings and weekend work in all weathers, the life is hard. It consists of mucking out, feeding and grooming and keeping the yard tidy, as well as the work with horses. The middle-aged 'lad' is an exception and the average age of jockeys and stable hands is 20–25. But the best stables are good places to work in, with a happy atmosphere and a sense of teamwork.

Getting in

About 50–60 boy and girl **apprentices** are taken on each year by one of the 1000 or so trainers licensed by the Jockey Club. Trainee jockeys must be good at handling as well as riding horses. Flat-race jockeys also have to be very light. The handicapping system is based on a weight of 7 stone 10 pounds, (7st 3lb if the apprentices' allowance is claimed). The figures over the jumps are 10 stone (or 9st 7lb for the allowance claim). The metric equivalents are 49 kg (46 kg with the claim) for the flat, and 63.5 kg (60.3 kg with the claim) over jumps.

The apprenticeship may last from five to seven years, but there is no guarantee of qualifying as a jockey. A trainee stops being an apprentice over the flat when he or she has ridden 95 winners or reaches the age of 25. The equivalent for jumps jockeys is 65 winners or age 26.

The Racing and Thoroughbred Breeding Training Board (RTBTB) runs NVQs/SNVQs at three levels. At an early stage, most apprentices attend one of two specialist training courses, at Newmarket and Doncaster.

Vince Coogan – National Hunt rider

Vince is 19 and in his second year of National Hunt riding. His father was a professional jumps jockey and Vince wanted a similar career from the age of about 13. Instead of becoming a 'pupil assistant', he stayed at school to pass three A levels, while continuing to ride at point-to-point races.

I joined a trainer's stables after A levels and had 12 rides in my first year. I need 15 winners to lose my 7 lb claim and hope to do this over the next two years (7lb is 3.18kg).

I enjoy the life. Every day's different and I like working with animals. The most difficult thing is the 'wasting', the effort to always keep your weight down.

My advice to would-be jockeys is 'Get the best education you can, so that you've got something to fall back on. Then, just give it your best shot.'

There is an alternative 'amateur' path into National Hunt racing, where entrants do not follow a formalized training scheme. This is the path taken by many successful jump jockeys, including Richard Dunwoody and Peter Scudamore.

The RTBTB publishes *Careers in Racing*.

Motor cycling

There are fewer than 300 or so professionals, in either road or speedway branches of the sport. In the UK, professional riders tend to combine racing with associated work in **manufacturing**, **dealing** or cycle **repair**. The top **speedway riders** can also ride abroad, where earnings can be higher.

Getting in

As with most sports, you have to work your way through the amateur ranks, via scrambling or grass-tracking (speedway on grass). Only the most talented make it at professional level, as a member of a speedway track racing team.

Opportunities in motorcycle sport and leisure in Britain are dealt with by the Auto-Cycle Union. This is also the body that issues licences to speedway riders.

Motor racing

Motor racing is a major export earner for Britain and attracts massive sponsorship, with a global TV audience that may reach 350 million for Formula One races.

The motor sport industry employs about 150,000 people either full- or part-time in Britain, with most working in support functions. There are opportunities in **design**, **testing** and **manufacture**, as well as in the higher-profile motor sport teams themselves. Other jobs are found in race and rally **driving schools**, and in **media** and **public relations** work.

There are only about 100 **drivers** from the UK employed on a full-time basis in the various motor sport fields, including Formula One and rally driving. All have to be licensed by the RAC (Royal Automobile Club).

⭐ *Young karters taste competition in the British Karting Grand Prix at Silverstone.*

Getting in

Most drivers start in **kart racing**, where you can drive competitively from as early as eight years old. Formula One champions Nigel Mansell and Michael Schumacher both came into the sport this way. Be aware that it can be quite a struggle to fund your way through an expensive sport like motor racing.

It is best at an early stage to join one of the 700 recognized motor clubs: the Motor Sports Association (MSA) can provide details and advice about these clubs. The MSA covers all branches of motor sport, with the exception of stock car racing, grass track racing and motor cycling (see separate entry for last of these).

Several further education colleges run courses relevant to the motor sport industry. Loughborough University, Oxford Brookes University and Swansea Institute of Higher Education offer degree courses. All the courses are listed in the MSA's directory, *Go Motor Sport*.

Outdoor pursuits

There are career opportunities in a range of activities, including climbing, orienteering, horse riding and watersports, often as an **instructor** or **activity leader**.

There are now few opportunities for specialist teachers of outdoor pursuits in schools. Outdoor education and environmental centres use qualified teachers as **managers**, while qualified instructors deliver specialist activities. Riding schools and riding holiday centres also use qualified instructors.

In some holiday centres, activity leaders are concerned with leisure holidays rather than coaching performance. A number of organizations specialize in activity holidays and courses that provide challenges for individuals or groups. They employ staff as **development trainers** to supervise the challenges.

Instructors help young people through coastal waters on a 'coasteering' expedition.

Much of the work is of a part-time or seasonal nature and some young people start by taking on voluntary work. The pay of instructors, activity leaders and development trainers varies, depending on the work and the type of organization.

The manager of a local authority outdoor education centre, normally teacher-trained, is paid on the standard teacher pay scale and can earn in the region of £18,000–£25,000 a year.

CONSIDER THIS...

FURTHER AND HIGHER EDUCATION QUALIFICATIONS INCLUDE:
- BED/BA COURSE IN OUTDOOR EDUCATION
- SPORTS SCIENCE/STUDIES DEGREES WITH OUTDOOR EDUCATION SPECIALISM (BANGOR, CENTRAL LANCASHIRE)
- BTEC/SQA NATIONAL AND HIGHER NATIONAL COURSES

Getting in

Instructors' qualifications are vital for those leading or teaching outdoor pursuits. NVQs/SVQs are replacing existing qualifications, but each activity has its own body which oversees training. For example, the Mountain Leader Training Board runs mountain leader and instructor courses, and the International Mountain Guide qualification means the instructor can take people on mountaineering expeditions abroad. The British Horse Society runs professional qualifications in the equestrian sector. Other basic qualifications include the Central Council of Physical Recreation's (CCPR) Community Sports Leaders Award, Hanson Leadership Award and the Basic Expedition Training Award.

A teaching qualification is useful and essential for some careers, but any degree needs to be supported by specialist instructor awards.

Even while still at school, you can prepare for a possible career in this field. Schools and other outside organizations may offer the opportunity to undertake sports leadership courses or one of the Duke of Edinburgh awards. First aid training could be an important first step, since a basic qualification is essential, right across this area of work.

Further information is available in most cases from the individual specialist organization or controlling body for each type of activity. Many are listed at the back of the book.

Rugby

Professional playing opportunities have increased in recent years, with the opening up of rugby union to commercial influences. Rugby league, with its history as a professional sport (with approximately 1600 professional players), is not as wealthy at top level and still has many part-time players who have other jobs. There is now some crossing over of the traditional boundaries between the union and league games.

Getting in

All professional clubs in both disciplines have scouts who visit schools and amateur matches. Many rugby league clubs run training schemes for apprentices, some of whom are offered a professional contract at the age of 17.

The Rugby Football Union, the governing body for rugby union, is considering the establishment of national youth academies to equip 12- to 21-year-olds with life skills and an education programme to serve them outside the game. The RFU already has 54 full-time Youth Development Officers, with broad responsibilities for furthering the interests of the game. It also runs Proficiency Award Schemes, which allow young people to assess their progress.

⭐ *For these New Zealand schoolboys, rugby is the premier sport.*

Squash

Britain's success at the top level in recent years has not meant any significant progress in squash as a media sport. It has proved difficult to market the sport through TV and it does not lend itself to large live audiences for competitions or exhibitions. Despite its continuing popularity as a participation sport, squash does not therefore support many professionals.

Getting in

The only way in is through excelling as a player of the amateur game and eventually reaching the elite levels, where there are some financial rewards.

Table tennis

Table tennis became one of the first open sports in the UK, when it removed the distinction between amateur and professional players.

There are only a handful of full-time players in the UK, and they form part of the national squad. Several of the English squad members live at the Table Tennis Institute at Holme Pierrepoint in Nottingham.

Opportunities are slightly greater in mainland Europe, where there are professional and semi-professional leagues, such as the German Bundesliga.

Getting in

You need to play in one of the leagues run by local table tennis associations. There is also a thriving tournament circuit, where young players can make their mark. It is essential to make an impact at an early age: all the top players have excelled at local and county level by the time they are aged 13 or 14.

Tennis

Tennis became an open sport largely through player pressure and players have more say in its running than in many other sports. It is one of the big business sports, which means there are more career opportunities. Apart from the elite few who make it onto the Association of Tennis Professionals (ATP) Tour, there are many other opportunities in **coaching** and **administration**. The Lawn Tennis Association (LTA) itself employs some 200 people in **training**, coaching and **development**; in **organizing** events and tournaments; in **officiating**; and in **finance** and **administration**.

Tim Henman

Tim Henman recognizes that there might have been some sacrifices in leaving school at 16 and missing out on a university education. *'But, if there are any sacrifices, I'm sure the positives far outweigh the negatives'.* Tim Henman is one of sport's millionaires but he claims that, *'Money has never been the major factor.'*

⭐ *Tim Henman made rapid progress from local club tennis to a place in the top ten world rankings.*

Getting in

Almost all the top players started playing at a very early age. Progress is usually from local club to the county squad and team. The best players are then selected to take part in one of the national squads – for younger players these operate at under-12, under-14 and under-16 levels. Squad training takes place at the LTA's National Tennis Centre at Bisham Abbey.

HAVE YOU THOUGHT OF...

● APPLYING FOR A TENNIS SCHOLARSHIP IN THE USA? STUDYING ALONGSIDE INTER-COLLEGIATE COMPETITION SUITS SOME PEOPLE. YOU NEED TO WEIGH UP THE OPTIONS CAREFULLY. FURTHER INFORMATION IS AVAILABLE FROM THE LTA AND FROM COLLEGE PROSPECTS OF AMERICA.

Scholarships and subsidies are offered by some schools in the independent and state sectors. In Surrey, Cheam High School runs a scholarship scheme at sixth form level. Other schools offering tennis scholarships include Millfield (Somerset), Repton (Derbyshire), Queenswood (Hertfordshire) and Sir Hugh Owen (Gwynedd, Wales).

The LTA has scholarship agreements with several British universities – Bath, Leeds Metropolitan, Loughborough, Stirling and University of Wales Institute. Several other universities have a strong background in tennis; these include Exeter, Middlesex, Nottingham and Teesside. Greenwich University has a degree course in Sports Science with Professional Tennis Coaching. There is also a wide range of education and training opportunities on the administration side, including a degree course in Recreational Management & Tennis at Buckingham University.

How to break in

The last chapter included information about getting into individual sports as a player. Now for some more general information about education and training and how it relates to careers in sport.

You will have seen that, in many sports, progression is through first becoming a top-class amateur. For many more, a structured education/training route is a must. Generally, the best advice is to gain a good foundation of general education. In some sports and sports-related careers, an apprenticeship or traineeship (usually with relatively low pay levels) is available direct from school at the age of 16. This may be linked with formal qualifications (see 'Work-based route' on page 34).

Level 4/5	Degree Courses Higher National Diploma/Certificate			NVQ and SVQ Level 5 NVQ and SVQ Level 4	
Level 3	A & AS levels or International Baccalaureate	Advanced GNVQ	BTEC National Diploma	NVQ and SVQ Level 3 (Modern Apprenticeship)	Scottish Highers
Level 2	5 GCSEs Grades A–C	Intermediate GNVQ	BTEC First Diploma/ SQA National Certificate Modules	NVQ and SVQ Level 2 Traineeships & National Traineeships	Scottish Standard Grade Credit/ Intermediate 2
Level 1	GCSE Grade D–G	Foundation GNVQ		NVQ and SVQ Level 1	Scottish Standard Grade General/ Intermediate 1

⭐ *This chart shows the range of qualifications at different levels.*

You are more likely to be carrying on at school/college until 18 and taking GCSEs, AS levels, A levels or GNVQs/GSVQs, Scottish Standard or Higher Grades, or other qualifications. Some sixth forms offer GNVQs in Leisure and Recreation (Advanced) or Leisure and Tourism (Intermediate and Foundation): the Intermediate GNVQ is equivalent to four or five GCSEs at grades A–C, while the Advanced GNVQ is worth at least two A levels. As well as the GNVQ, colleges of further education may offer other relevant courses, such as those for City & Guilds qualifications. All these are listed in the *Directory of Further Education* published by CRAC/Hobsons.

Specialist sports colleges

You may be studying at one of the 34 secondary schools with Specialist Sports College status. Or you might be interested in finding out whether there is such a college near you and if it could help you in your own sporting progress. These are schools which have a strong record in sports development, together with good academic standards, and they attract additional funding from the government. Each specialist sports college has a focus on certain sports.

This table tennis lesson is taking place in the sports hall at Barking Abbey School.

Work-based route

For some, there is the alternative of a more work-based training route from age 16, perhaps with NVQs/SVQs as the qualification route. NVQs are available at levels 1–4 in Sports and Recreation, which often involves some college study along with work-based assessment. You can also take an NVQ through a Modern Apprenticeship (in Scotland part of the Skillseekers Initiative) or a National Traineeship in sports-related areas, for example in Motor Sport. Modern Apprenticeships are for those who have the ability to work to NVQ level 3 or higher.

The British Sports Trust oversees **sports leader** courses throughout the UK. Many use the qualification in voluntary posts and some proceed into related employment. The Keep Fit Association offers courses that include nationally recognized qualifications and the chance to gain NVQs/SVQs in Movement and Dance Fitness.

Other options include NEBSM courses and the Diploma in Youth and Community Work. In England and Wales, the Diploma has a minimum entry age of 23 and entry requirements include relevant experience. In Scotland candidates enter from 18, with minimum requirements of four S grades (1–3) and two H grades, including English.

Higher education

For some professional players and a high proportion of those involved in sports-related careers, higher education is the first step. With something like 50 per cent of the population now taking a degree, graduate status is a baseline requirement for many levels of employment in sport.

There are about 40–50 degree courses in sports science, sports studies, or other leisure-related subjects in the UK. That's quite apart from many other courses in physical education or human movement studies for those who want to teach in schools or colleges.

There are well-established sports-related degree courses at many universities. Some offer sponsorship opportunities or bursaries. These include Bath, Birmingham, Bristol, Brunel, Cardiff, Glasgow, Kent (cricket and rugby), Loughborough, Manchester, Nottingham, Queen's Belfast, Portsmouth, Stirling and University College Worcester (cricket, netball and rugby only). Many other courses focus more broadly on leisure management. For those who want to keep their options open, sports and leisure studies can be combined with many other subjects. At postgraduate level, Loughborough University has an MBA in Sport & Leisure – one of the prestigious Master's courses that are highly valued by modern business.

Some of these universities are also National Network England sites – specialist centres linked to the headquarters of the UK Sports Institute at Sheffield.

Dalebank Books' *The Potter Guide to Higher Education* gives up-to-date information about the facilities available at each institution of higher education – both on campus and at nearby centres of excellence, such as Olympic-standard swimming pools and outdoor pursuit facilities. It also tells you the top-performing institutions in British University Sports Association (BUSA) competition, a useful indication of how seriously sport is taken at each university. The most successful universities include Birmingham, Durham (men), Edinburgh, Exeter (men), Loughborough, Nottingham, Oxford (women) and University of Wales Institute Cardiff.

⭐ *Stirling University offers more than 20 sports scholarships to talented young people.*

Stirling University

Stirling offers scholarships in sports ranging from athletics and badminton to canoeing and swimming. Scholarship holders have the option of an additional year's study at no extra cost to complete their degrees. Each scholarship of about £1500 allows a student to take part in senior competition – for which they receive specialist coaching. Scholarship holders are allowed no concessions: they have to achieve the same admissions requirements as other students.

Scotland also has a range of HNC/HND programmes in sports-associated areas such as Sports Coaching and Development, as well as in Leisure and Recreation Management. As with university degree courses, the practical content of each course and the emphasis on sporting ability varies from institution to institution.

There has also been an increase in the number of BTEC/SQA Higher National courses in Leisure Studies and related subjects. These provide an alternative to degree courses at a marginally lower level (in terms of entry requirements). Colleges of further and higher education offer HNC/HND courses and there are sometimes links that enable students to proceed on to degrees.

More sources of information

Use these publications to carry out careful research into the details of style and content, assessment and entrance requirements for the different courses offered:

- *Official Guide to University and College Entrance* (UCAS)
- *Entrance Guide to Higher Education in Scotland* (COSHEP/UCAS)
- *Handbook of Initial Teacher Training* (NATFHE)
- *Degree Course Guide for Leisure & Sports Studies* (CRAC/Hobsons)
- *Degree Course Guides* – for individual subjects, including sport (CRAC/Hobsons)
- *Laser Compendium of Higher Education* (Butterworth Heinemann)
- *Choosing your Degree Course and University* (Trotman)
- *How to Choose your HND course* (Trotman)
- *Which Degree?* (CRAC/Hobsons)
- *What Do Graduates Do?* (UCAS/CSU)
- *Which University?* and *ECCTIS 2000*, the UK courses information computer database, which is also available on CD-ROM
- UCAS website: www.ucas.ac.uk

⭐ *Don't forget the careers library as a source of information about careers and higher education.*

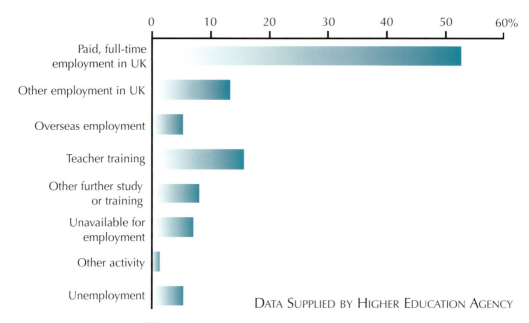

| | 0 | 10 | 20 | 30 | 40 | 50 | 60% |

Paid, full-time employment in UK

Other employment in UK

Overseas employment

Teacher training

Other further study or training

Unavailable for employment

Other activity

Unemployment

DATA SUPPLIED BY HIGHER EDUCATION AGENCY

⭐ *This block chart shows the first destinations of graduates in sports, leisure and recreation in 1996, as given by the* CRAC Degree Course Guide for Sport and Leisure.

The new national training organization for the sports and leisure industry (SPRITO) has published *Sport, Recreation & Allied Occupations – How to Get In.* This is intended primarily as a guide for college and university students, but contains a lot of information of interest to those thinking about a career in sport or recreation at a younger age.

Remember to seek guidance from the careers adviser working with your own school or college and to get in touch with the governing body of your chosen sport to see what information they can provide. When writing to these governing bodies or other organizations, it is best to include a stamped addressed A4 sized envelope.

Sports-related jobs and careers

The vast majority of those working in the sports and leisure industry are not professional sports players. Some are semi-professionals, able to supplement their main income with extra earnings from active participation in sport. Far more are recreational participants only, but earning their living from a sports-related job or career. There are many full-time jobs in areas such as sports administration and development.

Teaching

In secondary schools, specialist **teachers** of PE, games and dance/movement normally teach at least one other subject, usually one for which they are qualified through their degree course. They also take the main responsibility for coaching school teams and taking them to matches and other competitive events.

At primary level, the class teacher normally teaches games, PE and movement. Some primary teachers do more games and PE than others. Male teachers still tend to be in demand to take football, although many women now also take on this role.

In independent schools, sport is usually high profile and this can bring chances of greater specialization (although, as with state sector schools, PE and games teachers often offer an additional subject). Some of the larger independent schools even employ professional **coaches** to oversee training and competition for particular sports, such as rowing or rugby.

PE teachers are paid on the standard teachers' scale, earning approximately £14,000–£30,000.

⭐ *Hockey is played in nearly every secondary school.*

Getting in

To teach in state sector schools, you normally need a teacher training qualification. This is obtained by taking either a specialist teacher training degree course (a BEd degree) or a degree with Qualified Teacher Status (QTS) or by taking a degree course followed by a Post-Graduate Certificate in Education (PGCE). You might want to consider taking a Sports Science or Sports Studies degree before taking the PGCE. In fact, there are quite a few alternatives within the two main options and, if considering teaching as a career, you should seek guidance on the choice. Your careers teacher or careers adviser can offer an overview, while your PE teachers will be able to tell you how they set about qualifying.

Don't forget that there are demanding academic requirements for all those who wish to teach. To enter a degree course, you'll need at least two A levels, or four AS levels, or an Advanced GNVQ (or the equivalent), plus a range of GCSEs that include Mathematics and English at grade C or above (and Science for would-be primary teachers). Although a training qualification is not a requirement in independent schools, most teachers in this sector are also trained and qualified.

Coaching, instruction and training

Coaching and **instructing** take place in sports clubs, outdoor pursuit centres, sports and leisure centres, colleges and universities, gyms and health clubs. It is also often part of a more general sports role in organizations such as hotels, or holiday and fitness centres.

Team coaching has always had a high profile, but there are increasing opportunities for those working with individuals or groups. Local authorities are working with the National Coaching Foundation (NCF) to develop coaching as part of their sports development strategy and this is opening up new opportunities for coaching.

Much coaching is unpaid, with the situation varying greatly between sports. Athletics has a tradition of expert coaching but few paid coaches, whereas tennis coaching is often on a paid basis, even at quite junior levels. Where coaches are paid, it is most often on a part-time basis, so coaching can be combined with a completely separate career or used to build up a portfolio of work. In some of the bigger sports, more substantial contracts, sometimes full-time, are available with national governing bodies and with professional clubs.

⭐ *The coach is working with young footballers at soccer's Youth Academy.*

Getting in

Coaches need to hold the appropriate awards for their individual sport. Each governing body runs its own award scheme. For some coaches working more generally, this means qualifying at basic level across a range of sports. For others, it means specializing in one sport and working up through the levels of award.

There are degree courses for those seeking a broad-based foundation. Sports Coaching & Development courses are run at several universities. Liverpool John Moores has Coaching Science, Nottingham Trent has Sport and Sports Science with Coaching. HND courses include those at Southwark College and Stockport College. The many higher education courses in Sports Science, Movement Studies or Physical Education also offer a good basis for coaching.

The NCF runs a programme of coaching courses across most sports and at all levels. The NCF Award in Coaching Studies develops basic knowledge and understanding of the principles and practice of sports coaching. The Certificate in Coaching Studies is for those already practising as coaches and who want to progress through a nationally recognized qualification. The NCF now also has a part-time degree course in Applied Sports Coaching, validated by Leicester's De Montfort University, but this is meant for experienced coaches.

There are NVQs/SNVQs (levels 1–3) in Sport, Recreation and Allied Industries, which include Coaching, Teaching and Instructing, but these do not cover all sports.

The armed forces also employ physical instructors and officers. In the RAF recruits are trained as instructors or officers, while the Army and Royal Navy recruit their instructors from their serving members.

If you are interested in coaching/tuition, remember to look for your particular sport in 'Earning from playing' (pages 8–31).

Health and fitness training

This is a wide field, including aerobics, gymnastics, keep fit, weightlifting and exercise to music. Many **trainers** specialize in a particular activity, such as step aerobics or trampolining. **Exercise** and **fitness professionals** are often self-employed. They build up their own portfolio of work, which may mean booking facilities and running courses or classes, as well as taking sessional employment with a range of employers. The work is mostly with groups, but can also be with individual clients. It can mean quite a lot of travel and variable working hours. Full-time posts are salaried at a similar rate to leisure assistants (in the region of £8000–£12,000 a year). Self-employed **fitness instructors** are most often paid at an hourly rate.

Getting in

There is no formal structure for progression in this field and success depends on the reputation you can build as an instructor. But you do need to obtain the awards and qualifications for your specialist activity and the level at which you are teaching. NVQs/SNVQs are being developed to replace existing qualifications in health and fitness training.

British Gymnastics has a comprehensive coaching and qualifications structure. A training programme is provided for coaches at five levels, from Assistant Coach up through to International Performance Coach. Scotland has Fitness Scotland to administer training courses in all branches of exercise and dance fitness.

Debbie — Fitness Instructor

Debbie works part-time as a fitness instructor and lifestyle consultant. She teaches aerobics, step and circuit classes and helps people with personal fitness programmes.

I did teacher training, but decided I'd prefer to work in the fitness industry, so I took an intensive 10-week course with Premier Training. The course was module-based, and covered biomechanics, testing, lifestyle management, exercise to music, and massage.

I started with some shift work in a leisure centre gym. Now I set up other sessions myself – community education classes and in village halls. I made a positive choice to work part-time and like the flexibility. I like to have time for myself and know I could always increase the working hours. I like the variety, meeting new people and helping them assess and develop their personal fitness. It's not so good when you're not feeling 100% or have got an injury and the hours can sometimes be a bit unsociable. You've really got to want to do it, otherwise it shows.

My advice for young people includes the need to be business-minded. You've got to be prepared to pay for courses, and then there's insurance and tax. I went on a self-employment seminar run by the local Training & Enterprise Council before starting up on my own. The TEC can also sometimes help with Career Development Loans.

⭐ *A fitness instructor may take many different activities including step aerobics.*

Sports administration

This field includes those who run their sport and those who work to **develop** sport in the community. It also covers work in **fundraising** and **sponsorship** and **event co-ordination**. With the strong traditions for amateur sport, many sports have well-established structures which still rely on volunteer administrators. However, the move towards professionalization in many sports is increasing the need for full-time **administrative staff**.

See also 'Sports and leisure centres' (page 47) and 'Sports development' (page 49).

Getting in

There is no overall requirement for specific qualifications in this field, but the higher the position and salary, the more likely it is you will need formal qualifications. City & Guilds offers the Certificate in Management of Recreation & Leisure Environments, while BTEC has courses in Leisure Studies, Leisure Management and Travel & Tourism. In Scotland SQA offers similar courses. Many schools and colleges offer the GNVQ in Leisure and Tourism (Leisure and Recreation at Advanced level), though it is important to realize that GNVQ courses provide a broad introduction to the whole occupational sector rather than a specific vocational qualification.

There are many degree and postgraduate courses available in Sports Science and Sports Studies (see previous chapter). While any degree is helpful, a degree in a sports- or business-related subject will give you a particularly good start.

The Institute of Leisure and Amenity Management (ILAM) and the Institute of Sport and Recreation Management (ISRM) offer a range of professional qualifications.

Sports clothing and equipment

The **manufacture** and **supply** of sports clothing and equipment is a significant industry in its own right. Design, manufacture and retail bring job opportunities for **designers**, **technical** and **administrative staff** and **marketing** and **sales staff**. In all these areas, a knowledge of, and interest in, sport is valuable. Some of the work is part-time, with people supplementing their income (which may come from active involvement in sport) by selling or repairing bikes or tennis rackets, for example.

Getting in

It's hard to generalize about entry. Some people have degrees in Textile Science or Technology, others have come from a playing background. Degree courses to explore include those in Sports Equipment Design at Central Lancashire, Glamorgan and Salford Universities, Sports & Materials Science (Birmingham University, Sport & Exercise Science & Textiles (Bolton Institute) and Sports Product Design (South Bank University, London). Sheffield Hallam University offers an HND course, while Leicester South Fields University has an HNC in Sports and Leisurewear Design.

⭐ Chris Boardman broke the world hour record in 1996 with a distance of 56.375 km. His bicycle was made from state-of-the-art materials and his clothes were designed to give minimal air resistance.

Grounds maintenance and sports turf management

There are openings for **greenkeepers** and **grounds maintenance staff** at sports clubs and leisure centres. The work has become increasingly sophisticated and you need to have a good working knowledge of turf technology, soil fertilizers and irrigation techniques.

Getting in

At lower levels, it is possible to work in the area without formal qualifications. To qualify as a senior or head groundsman, you need suitable qualifications and experience in ground construction work, turf maintenance and preparation, soil care and some horticultural work.

Sports and leisure centres

There are now about 1500–1600 sports and leisure centres in the UK. In addition to the centres run by local authorities, there are privately owned health and fitness studios and gyms/leisure clubs attached to hotels and country clubs. Some specialist sports clubs, for example football or squash, also offer fitness facilities to supplement their own specialism. This trend is likely to continue, as the UK moves towards continental models of sports provision. Some large holiday centres also offer employment opportunities related to sports.

The jobs range from **assistant** to **management level**. **Managers** are involved with planning sports and exercise programmes, special events, organizing publicity, staff issues, budgets, building and equipment maintenance, and health and safety. **Assistants** set up and move equipment and demonstrate its safe use, supervise activities, assist at classes and fitness sessions, do lifeguarding and other duties in the pool, and deal with bookings and enquiries. In the smaller organizations, all staff are likely to take on a wide range of tasks.

⭐ *An instructor coaches a group of young divers.*

Managers can expect to earn in the range of £12,000–£25,000, dependent on levels of experience and seniority. Sports and leisure assistants may earn around £8000–£12,000.

Getting in

There are many different routes into sports and leisure management, but most managers have followed a recognized progression route within the occupational area.

Many organizations operate trainee manager schemes, recruiting either directly from the higher education institutions or through the general or specialist leisure media. Very often people enter the industry at a lower level and work their way up to management levels, taking appropriate qualifications along the way. Flexibility and adaptability are important. The work is demanding, with shiftwork normal. An appreciation of good customer services practice is needed at all levels.

There are also post-graduate qualifications, suitable both for those who have sports-related degrees and for those who have followed unrelated degrees.

CONSIDER THIS...

COURSES AND TRAINING PROGRAMMES INCLUDE:
- DEGREE COURSES IN SPORTS & RECREATION, LEISURE MANAGEMENT, ETC
- BTEC/SQA HIGHER NATIONAL COURSES IN LEISURE STUDIES
- NVQs/SVQs IN SPORTS & RECREATION
- MODERN APPRENTICESHIPS (SKILLSEEKERS INITIATIVE IN SCOTLAND) IN SPORTS & RECREATION

Other useful qualifications for those who want to work in sports centres include first aid and the RLSS National Pool Lifeguard Qualification. Coaching qualifications in particular sports, such as badminton, gymnastics, swimming and table tennis, are also helpful in a very competitive field. If working as a centre assistant, you are likely to be asked to work for other qualifications, often those run by ILAM (project-based, at four levels) or ISRM (module-based).

At school or college level, you might consider the GNVQ/GSVQ route. The GNVQs/GSVQs in Business and in Leisure & Tourism provide a broad base of studies that are relevant in different ways to aspects of sports and leisure work.

Sports development

Local authorities, sporting governing bodies and the regional and national sports councils are all employers. Most work at this level involves **sports development officers** in a full range of sports, but there is some specialism in the larger authorities.

As well as promoting sport, development work may include funding and sponsorship – both the raising and allocation of money. It involves contact with the general public, people from other sporting bodies, and with local and national government. Skills and experience are frequently transferable – the UK Athletics Development Officer (at time of publication) previously worked for the Lawn Tennis Association.

Sports development officers might expect to earn around £12,000–£16,000 early in their career. More senior development officers will earn in the range of £18,000–£35,000.

Getting in

Sports development work usually requires a higher education qualification or experience in sports-related work. As with sports administration, any degree may be helpful, while there are many sports-related degree courses that provide a good way in. Many senior people working in this field have postgraduate qualifications, for example the MA in Leisure Management.

Other courses available include BTEC National and Higher National (or Scottish equivalents) and City & Guilds. The ISRM offers on-the-job training. There are also NVQs/SNVQs.

The first job is often hard to get as this is a competitive field. However, once you do make it, prospects are good. There is a lot of movement up the scale, as people take more senior posts.

Mark Miles – Deputy Stadium Manager

Mark is a successful athlete. He has good GCSEs and took four A levels. But he did not enjoy sixth form studies and could not see where they were leading him. He managed two passes and took a place on the HND in Sports Science at Crewe & Alsager.

It was a broad-based course with a good mix of theoretical and practical studies. The course gave me a new motivation. I passed with a distinction and went on to a degree course, choosing the Business, Sport & Recreation option. Although the competition for a first job is very strong, I landed a job with a local authority to start the day after I graduated!

After a few years in this job, Mark moved on to his present job, working in one of the country's leading athletics stadiums. The work remains demanding and Mark can expect to work some evenings and weekends.

I have to be well organized, planning activities several months in advance. A lot of the work involves liaison with the governing bodies. Every day is different, I never come in and do the same thing. You are being paid for something you enjoy doing and it's a very sociable job. The only downside is that sport invades your life and is no longer just relaxation. And the pay's not too good in the early stages!

Mark has a number of basic coaching and instruction awards. He is also a Club Coach in Athletics and has taken a National Coaching Federation (NCF) introductory course. Other training through his local authority employer has included courses in basic management, first aid, risk assessment and IT. In the longer term, he would like to take a Master's degree in a sports-related subject.

⭐ *A good educational background followed by further training and experience has led to a challenging and fulfilling career as a deputy stadium manger for Mark Miles.*

Sports dietetics and nutrition

This is a small but growing field. Sports people in particular are becoming more conscious that they 'are what they eat'. At top competitive levels, in particular, the high standards demand attention to good dietary strategies and nutritional habits. Openings are mainly in the independent sector, with **dieticians** and **nutritionists** often working only part-time in the sports-specific field.

Getting in

To qualify as a dietician, you need a degree in Human Nutrition within the State Registration in Dietetics scheme. There are also postgraduate Dietetics courses. After at least one year's practical experience, you can apply for a course in Sports Dietetics, run by the Sports Nutrition Foundation and validated by the British Dietetic Association.

Sports medicine and therapy

Sports therapy treatment includes massage, heat and hydrotherapy, but **sports therapists** also advise on exercise and training programmes. **Physiotherapists**, **sports masseurs** and **remedial therapists** all work in this field. Some **osteopaths** and other specialist practitioners also choose to treat sports-related injuries. A few doctors also specialize in sports medicine and therapy.

Physiotherapists earn in the range £13,000–£28,000. Osteopaths' pay varies, but is similar to physiotherapists. **Fitness instructors** are usually paid an hourly rate.

 *TV coverage has made this a familiar sight – the club physio treats an injured footballer.*

Getting in

Chartered physiotherapists are well qualified, needing a degree in physiotherapy. Entry to such courses now demands high grades at A level, usually including science subjects. Osteopaths also have a lengthy training, usually at degree level. Although the qualification route for masseurs is less structured, there are many courses of varying length. Truro College, Cornwall, runs a degree course in Sports Science & Injury Management. The International Institute of Sports Therapy offers sports therapy qualifications. A range of other courses is offered in both state sector and independent colleges.

Sports journalism and photography

There are relatively few full-time positions in the media that are specific to an individual sport. There are more in football, but even this is mainly at national level.

Getting in

Sports journalists often start as non-specialist journalists, but they may come from a background of active involvement in the sport. Many big name personalities become excellent journalists, although many others (especially those who remain active performers) have their articles written or 'ghosted' by specialist journalists. Edge Hill College runs a degree course in Sports Studies with Writing. Further information is available from the National Council for the Training of Journalists and from the Sports Writers Association.

Photographers need to do normal training as photographers. Some then specialize within a single sport.

What then?

Planning for life after an active sports career

Young people driven by a passion for sport tend not to plan for the time when their skills will no longer earn them a living. Even some of the more successful will not earn enough to maintain themselves (and their families) after the end of their active career in sport.

Are you hoping to be a professional sports player, but realize you also need some reserve options? The previous chapter contains information both for those who want to plan a second career and for those who want to do some realistic contingency planning.

Your action plan should allow for the possibility of a break in your career in sport, or even a premature end to it. Injuries apart, an active career in sport is a short one for most. On average, top competitors in the most physically exerting sports have retired by the age of about 35, with the prospect of another 50 years of active life ahead of them.

There are few openings for retired players to continue earning their living as sports personalities. Don't be fooled by the high profile of exceptions such as Sue Barker, Frank Bruno and Steve Cram. There are openings for retired players and the previous pages have described some of these. The entry under 'Coaching, instruction and training' (page 41) may be relevant. The Rover Cricket Coach Initiative is a scheme that enables former players to continue playing an active part in the game. The Professional Footballers' Association (PFA) also helps its members to take vocational training for their post-playing careers.

SPORT

⭐ Mark Druce, a semi-professional with Kidderminster Harriers, passed an NVQ2 in Accounts, with the course partly funded by the PFA. 'When I do finish playing football, I will be ready for a new career and leaving active sport behind will not be such a shock.'

Jobs for former players, apart from coaching and management, include work in sports centres, with regional or national sports organizations, or in public relations and sports promotion.

Alternative career planning is not only for the sports professionals. Even if you do not earn your living as a player, you need to ask yourself whether the physical demands of a sports-related job may prevent you pursuing this job throughout your active working life. PE teaching or aerobics instruction is still possible for 55-year-olds, but for some, enthusiasm dwindles as the body becomes more reluctant!

The best advice for second career and contingency planning is to invest in education and training. Consider how education and training opportunities might help you at every stage. Think about how best to add other strings to your bow, even while you are an active sports person. The lower paid (or part-time) sports person will have an even greater need to use part of their time preparing for the future in this way.

Go back to the 'How to break in' section to check your understanding of the overall picture. And remember the 'Getting in' information under the individual sports in the 'Earning from playing' section.

And finally … at all times, be positive – but realistic.

Useful information,

addresses & contacts

GENERAL SPORTS ORGANIZATIONS

English Sports Council/Sport England
16 Upper Woburn Place
London WC1H 0QP
Tel: 020 7273 1500
www.sportengland.org.uk

Scottish Sports Council
Caledonia House, South Gyle
Edinburgh EH12 9DQ
Tel: 0131 317 7200
www.sportscotland.org.uk

The Sports Council for Wales
Welsh Institute of Sport
Sophia Gardens
Cardiff CF1 9SW
Tel: 029 2030 0500
www.sports-council-wales.co.uk

Sports Council for Northern Ireland
House of Sport
Upper Malone Road
Belfast BT9 5LA
Tel: 028 9038 1222
www.sportsni.org

Central Council of Physical Recreation
Francis House, Francis Street
London SW1P 1DE
Tel: 020 7828 3163

SPECIFIC SPORTS

Athletics
UK Athletics
10 Harborne Road, Edgbaston
Birmingham B15 3AA
Tel: 0121 456 5098
www.ukathletics.org

Badminton
Badminton Association of England
National Badminton Centre
Bradwell Road, Loughton Lodge
Milton Keynes MK8 9LA
Tel: 01908 268400
www.baofe.co.uk

Scottish Badminton Union
Cockburn Centre, 40 Bogmoor Place
Glasgow G51 4TQ
Tel: 0141 445 1218
www.scotbadminton.demon.co.uk

Basketball
English Basketball Association
48 Bradford Road, Stanningley
Leeds LS28 6DF
Tel: 0113 2361166
www.basketballengland.org.uk

Billiards and Snooker
World Professional Billiards & Snooker Association
27 Oakfield Road
Clifton, Bristol BS28 2AT
Tel: 0117 3178200
www.snookernet.com

World Ladies Snooker Association
PO Box 16
Wisbech PE13 2ZX
Tel: 01945 588598

Boxing (Amateur)
Amateur Boxing Association
The National Sports Centre
Crystal Palace, London SE19 2BB
Tel: 020 8778 0251

Boxing (Professional)
British Boxing Board of Control
Jack Petersen House
52A Borough High Street
London SE1 1XW
Tel: 020 7403 5879
www.bbbofc.com

Canoeing
British Canoe Union
John Dudderidge House
Adbolton Lane, West Bridgford
Nottingham NG2 5AS
Tel: 0115 9821100
www.bcu.org.uk

Cricket
England Cricket Board
Lords Cricket Ground
London NW8 8QZ
Tel: 020 7432 1200
www-uk6.cricket.org

Women's Cricket
Lords Cricket Ground
London NW8 8QZ
Tel: 020 7289 5619
www-uk6.cricket.org

Cycling
British Cycling Federation
National Cycling Centre
Stuart Street
Manchester M11 4DQ
Tel: 0161 2302301
www.bcf.uk.com

Darts
British Darts Organisation
2 Pages Lane, Muswell Hill
London N10 1PS
Tel: 020 8883 5544
www.bdodarts.com

Equestrian sports
British Horse Society
Stoneleigh Deer Park
Kenilworth CV8 2XZ
Tel: 01926 707700
www.bhs.org.uk

Football
Football Association
16 Lancaster Gate
London W2 3LW
Tel: 020 7262 4542
www.the-fa.org

Football Association of Ireland
80 Merrion Square, Dublin 2
Republic of Ireland
Tel: 00353 1 6766864
www.fai.ie.org

Professional Footballers' Association
2 Oxford Court, Bishopsgate
Manchester M2 3WQ
Tel: 0161 236 0575
www.givemefootball.com

Football refereeing
Referees' Association
1 Westhill Road, Coundon
Coventry CV6 2AD
Tel: 024 7660 1701
www.footballreferee.org

Golf (Amateur)
English Golf Union
National Golf Centre
The Broadway
Woodhall Spa LN10 6PU
Tel: 01526 354500
www.englishgolfunion.org

English Ladies' Golf Association
Edgbaston Golf Club, Church Road,
Edgbaston, Birmingham B15 3TB
Tel: 0121 4562088

Golf (Professional)
Professional Golfers'
Association/Women's PGA
Centenary House, The Belfry
Sutton Coldfield B76 9PT
Tel: 01675 470333
www.pga.org.uk

Gymnastics
British Gymnastics
Ford Hall
Lilleshall National Sports Centre,
Newport, Shropshire TF10 9NB
Tel: 01952 820330
www.baga.co.uk

Hockey
English Hockey Association
The Stadium, Silbury Boulevard,
Milton Keynes MK9 1HA
Tel: 01908 544644
www.hockeyonline.co.uk

Horse racing
The British Horseracing Board
42 Portman Square
London W1H 6EN
Tel: 020 7396 0011
www.bhb.co.uk

Ice Hockey
British Ice Hockey Association
The Galleries of Justice, Shire Hall
High Pavement, The Lace Market
Nottingham NG1 1HN
Tel: 0115 915 9204
www.icehockeyuk.co.uk

Judo
British Judo Association
7A Rutland Street
Leicester LE1 1RB
Tel: 0116 2559669
www.britishjudo.org.uk

Life Saving
Royal Life Saving Society
River House, High Street
Broom, Warwicks B50 4HN
Tel: 01789 773994
www.lifesavers.org.uk

Martial Arts
National Association of Karate &
Martial Arts schools
Rosecraig
Bullockstone Road
Herne Bay, Kent CT6 7NL
Tel: 01227 370055
www.nakmas.org.uk

Motor Cycling
Auto-Cycle Union
ACU House, Wood Street
Rugby CV21 2YX
Tel: 01788 566400
www.acu.org.uk

Motor Racing
RAC Motor Sports Association
Motor Sports House, Riverside Park
Colnbrook, Berks SL3 0HG
Tel: 01753 681736
www.rac.co.uk

Mountaineering
**Association of Mountaineering
Instructors**
Capel Curig
Gwynedd LL24 0ET
Tel: 01690 720314
www.ami.org

British Mountain Guides
Capel Curig
Gwynedd LL24 0ET
Tel: 01690 720314
www.bmg.org.uk

Mountain Leader Training Board
Capel Curig
Conwy LL24 0ET
Tel: 01690 720248
www.mltb.org

**Scottish Mountain Leader Training
Board**
Glenmore, Aviemore PH22 1QU
Tel: 01479 861248
www. members.aol.com/theukmtb

UK Mountain Training Board
Capel Curig
Gwynedd LL24 0ET
Tel: 01690 720314
www. members.aol.com/theukmtb

Netball
All England Netball Association
Netball House, 9 Paynes Park
Hitchin, Herts SG5 1EH
Tel: 01462 442344
www.england-netball.co.uk

Orienteering
British Orienteering Federation
Riversdale, Dale Road
North Darley Dale
Matlock DE4 2HX
Tel: 01629 734042
www.britishorienteering.org.uk

Outdoor Pursuits
Adventure Education Ltd
Eastgate House, Princesshay
Exeter EX1 1LY
Tel: 01392 272372
www.adventure-ed.co.uk

Institute for Outdoor Learning
12 St Andrews Churchyard
Penrith, Cumbria CA11 7YE
Tel: 01768 891065
www.outdoor-learning.org

**UK Institute for Careers and
Qualifications in the Outdoor
Industry**
c/o Tracey College (Exeter) Ltd,
Eastgate House, Princesshay
Exeter EX1 1LY
Tel: 01392 272372

Rugby League
**British Amateur Rugby League
Association**
West Yorkshire House
4 New North Parade
Huddersfield HD1 5JP
Tel: 01484 544131
www.barla.org.uk

Rugby Football League
Redhall House, Redhall Lane
Leeds LS17 8NB
Tel: 0113 232 9111
www.rfl.uk.com

Rugby Union
Irish Rugby Football Union
IRFU Grounds, 62 Landsdowne Road,
Dublin 4, Republic of Ireland
Tel: 00353 1 668 4601
Fax: 00353 1 660 5640
www.irfu.ie

Rugby Football Union
Rugby Road, Twickenham,
Middlesex TW1 1DX
Tel: 020 8892 2000
www.rfu.com

Scottish Rugby Union
Murrayfield
Edinburgh EH12 5PG
Tel: 0131 346 5000
www.sru.org.uk

Welsh Rugby Union
Custom House, Custom House Street
Cardiff CF10 1RF
Tel: 029 2078 1700
Fax: 029 2022 5601
www.wru.co.uk

Rugby Football Union for Women
Newbury RFC, Monks Lane
Newbury, Berks
Tel: 01635 42333

Sailing
Royal Yachting Association
RYA House, Romsey Road
Eastleigh, Hants SO50 9YA
Tel: 023 8062 7400
www.rya.org.uk

Skiing
British Association of Snowsport Instructors (BASI)
Glenmore, Aviemore PH22 1QU
Tel: 01479 861 717
Fax: 01479 861 718
www.basi.org.uk

English Ski Council
Area Library Building
Queensway Mall, The Cornbow
Halesowen B63 4AJ
Tel: 0121 5012314
www.englishski.org

Snowsport Scotland
Midlothian Ski Centre, Hillend
Biggar Road, Midlothian EH10 7EF
Tel: 0131 445 4151
Fax: 0131 445 4949
www.snsc.demon.co.uk

Squash
Squash Rackets Association
PO Box 52, Manchester M12 5FF
Tel: 0161 231 4499
Fax: 0161 231 4231
www.squash.co.uk

Sub-Aqua
British Sub-Aqua Club
26 Breckfield Road North
Liverpool L5 4NH
Tel: 0151 287 1001
www.saa.org.uk

Swimming
Amateur Swimming Association
Harold Fern House, Derby Square
Loughborough LE11 5AL
Tel: 01509 618719
www.swimming.org

Table Tennis
English Table Tennis Association
Queensbury House, 3rd Floor
Havelock Road
Hastings TN34 1HF
Tel: 01424 722 525
Fax: 01424 422 103
www.etta.co.uk

Scottish Table Tennis Association
Caledonia House, South Gyle
Edinburgh EH12 9DQ
Tel: 0131 317 8077
www.sol.co.uk/t/tabletennis/

Table Tennis Association of Wales
31 Maes-y-Celyn
Griffithstown, Pontypool
Torfaen NP4 5DG
Tel: 01495 756112
www.btinternet.com/~ttaw

Tennis
Lawn Tennis Association
Queen's Club
West Kensington
London W14 9EG
Tel: 020 7381 7000
www.lta.org.uk

Weightlifting
British Amateur Weight Lifters' Association
131 Hurst Street
Oxford OX4 1HE
Tel: 01865 200339
www.bawla.com

OTHER ORGANIZATIONS

Coaching
National Coaching Foundation
114 Cardigan Road
Headingley
Leeds LS6 3BJ
Tel: 0113 274 4802
Fax: 0113 275 5019
www.sportscoachuk.org

Opportunities for people with disabilities
British Sports Association for the Disabled
Solecast House
13–27 Brunswick Place
London N1 6DX
Tel: 020 8801 4466
www.britsport.com

British Amputees and Les Autres Sports Association
c/o 30 Greaves Close, Arnold
Nottingham NG5 6RS
Tel: 0115 9260220

British Blind Sport
67 Albert Street
Rugby CV21 2SN
Tel: 01788 536142

British Deaf Sports Council
7a Bridge Street
Otley, W. Yorks L21 1BQ
Tel: 01943 850214 (voice)
     01943 850081 (DCT)

British Wheelchair Sports Foundation
Guttmann Sports Centre, Harvey Road,
Stoke Mandeville, Aylesbury HP21 9PP
Tel: 01296 395 995

Scope (for people with cerebral palsy)
11 Churchill Park, Colwick
Nottingham NG4 2HF
Tel: 0115 940 1202
www.scope.org.uk

UK Sports Association for People with Learning Disability
Solecast House
13–27 Brunswick Place
London N1 6DX
Tel: 020 7250 1100

Education abroad
College Prospects of America (UK)
5 Manland Avenue
Harpenden AL5 4RE
Tel: 01582 712364
www.cpoauk.com

Examination bodies
Royal Society of Arts Examining Board
Westwood Way, Coventry CV4 8HS
Tel: 024 7647 0033
www.ocr.org.uk

First Aid
British Red Cross Society
9 Grosvenor Crescent
London SW1X 7EJ
Tel: 020 7235 5454
www.redcross.org.uk

St John's Ambulance
1 Grosvenor Crescent
London SW1X 7EF
Tel: 020 7235 5231
www.sja.org.uk

Grounds maintenance
National Playing Fields Association
Stanley House, St Chad's Place
London WC1X 9HH
Tel: 020 7833 5360
www.npfa.co.uk

Institute of Groundsmanship
19–23 Church Street
The Agora, Wolverton
Milton Keynes MK12 5LG
Tel: 01908 312511
www.iog.org

Health and fitness training
British Association of Sport and Exercise Sciences
114 Cardigan Road, Headingley
Leeds LS6 3BJ
Tel: 0113 2891020
www.bases.org.uk

Fitness Industry Association
5–11 Lavington Street
London SE1 0NZ
Tel: 020 7620 0700

Fitness Scotland
Caledonia House, South Gyle
Edinburgh EH12 9DQ
Tel: 0131 317 7243

The Fitness League
52 London Street
Chertsey KT16 8AJ
Tel: 01932 564567
www.thefitnessleague.com

Keep Fit Association
Astra House, Suite 1.05
Arklow Road, London SE14 6EB
Tel: 020 8692 9566
www.keepfit.org.uk

Higher education
Universities & Colleges Admissions Service (UCAS)
Rosehill, New Barn Lane
Cheltenham,]
 GL52 3LZ
Tel: 01242 227788
www.ucas.ac.uk

Leisure and amenity management
Institute of Leisure and Amenity Management
ILAM House, Lower Basildon
Reading RG8 9NE
Tel: 01491 874800
www.leisureopportunities.co.uk

Players agents
Association of Professional Sports Agents
Federation House, National Agricultural Centre, Stoneleigh Park Kenilworth CV8 2RF
Tel: 024 7641 4999
www.sportslife.org.uk

Sport and recreation management
Institute of Sport and Recreation Management
Giffard House, 36–38 Sherrard Street Melton Mowbray LE13 1XJ
Tel: 01664 565531
www.isrm.co.uk

Recreation Managers' Association of GB
Recreation House, 7 Burkinshaw Avenue, Rawmarsh
Rotherham S62 7QZ
Tel: 01709 522463

Sports administration
British Institute of Sports Administration
c/o The Lawn Tennis Association
The Queen's Club
Palliser Road
London W14 9EG
Tel: 020 7381 7000
www.lta.org.uk

Sports dietetics and nutrition
British Nutrition Foundation
High Holborn House
52–54 High Holborn
London WC1V 6RQ
Tel: 020 7404 6504
Fax: 020 7404 6747
www.nutrition.org.uk

Sports journalism
Sports Writers Association
c/o Sport England, External Affairs
16 Upper Woburn Place
London WC1H 0QP
Tel: 020 7273 1500

National Council for the Training of Journalists
Latton Bush Centre, Southern Way
Harlow CM18 7BL
Tel: 01279 430009
www.nctj.com

Sports massage and therapy
Fellowship of Sports Masseurs and Therapists
PO Box 81
Hertford SG13 8XW
Tel:01707 873698
www.fsmt~uk.org

National Sports Medicine Institute
32 Devonshire Street
London W1G 6PX
Tel: 020 7251 0583
Fax: 020 7251 0774
www.nsmi.org.uk

Sports physiotherapy
Association of Chartered Physiotherapists in Sports Medicine
Tel: 02920 744604

Sports therapy
Society of Sports Therapists
45C Carrick Street
Glasgow G2 8PJ
Tel: 0141 2213660
www.society-of-sports-therapists.org

Teaching
Physical Education Association of the UK
Ling House, Building 25
London Road
Reading RG1 5AQ
Tel: 0118 931 6240
Fax: 0118 931 6242
www.pea.uk.com

TRAINING IN THE SPORTS INDUSTRY

National Training Organisation for Sport, Recreation and allied Occupations (SPRITO)
24 Stephenson Way
London NW1 2HD
Tel: 020 7388 7755
www.sprito.org.uk and
www.sportsonline.co.uk

Women in sport
Women's Sports Foundation
305–315 Hither Green Lane
Lewisham
London SE13 6TJ
Tel: 020 8697 5370
www.wsf.org.uk

Get the jargon – a glossary of sports terms

ATP   Association of Tennis Professionals

BA   Bachelor of Arts – type of degree

BEd   Bachelor of Education – type of degree

biomechanics   the study of the mechanics of movement in living organisms

BTEC   Business and Technology Education Council (now part of Edexcel) – examination body for vocational qualifications

CCPR   central Council of Physical Recreation

City & Guilds   examination body for vocational qualifications

Club professional   employed by a golf club to run the shop, and teach and play with members ad visitors

COIC   Careers and Occupational Information Centre – careers information publisher

corporate activity   the involvement of business companies in entertaining their clients at major sporting events

COSHEP   Committee of Scottish Higher Education Principals

CRAC   Careers Research and Advisory Council – publisher in Careers and Higher Education

CSU   Central Services Unit – higher education publisher

distance learning   courses followed without attending the educational institution, e.g. TV or correspondence course

dietetics   the scientific study of diet and nutrition

ECCTIS   Educational Counselling and Credit Transfer Information Service – database of further and higher education courses.

funding   supply of money

GNVQ   General National Vocational Qualification

HNC   Higher National Certificate

HND   Higher National Diploma

ILAM   Institute of Leisure and Amenity Management

ISRM   Institute of Sport and Recreation Management

IT   Information Technology

LTA   Lawn Tennis Association – governing body for Tennis

marketing   Buying and selling

MBA Master of Business Administration – postgraduate degree

MCC Marylebone Cricket Club

merchandising trading in sports clothing and equipment

MSA Motor Sports Association

NATFHE National Association of Teachers in Further & Higher Education – teacher's association and publisher

NCF National Coaching Foundation

NEBSM National Examining Board for Supervisory Management

nutrition the study of food nutrients and energetics

NVQ National Vocational Qualification

PGA Professional Golfers' Association

PGCE Postgraduate Certificate in Education – teaching qualification

postgraduate a person who studies after obtaining a first degree

probationary period trial period to assess whether a person is suited to a job

public relations promotion of an organization or product (or sport)

RAC Royal Automobile Club

RFU Rugby Football Union

RLSS Royal Life Saving Society

RSA Royal Society of Arts – examination body for vocational qualifications

scholarship educational funding awarded for achievements or abilities

sessional employment work in coaching and instruction organized and paid on the basis of individual sessions

sponsorship funding or other support for sporting activities from business or other organizations

Sport England trading name of English Sports Council

SPRITO National Training Organisation for Sport, Recreation and allied Occupations

SQA Scottish Qualifications Authority

SVQ Scottish Vocational Qualification

UCAS Universities and Colleges Admissions Service

Index

SPORT